Unit 1

T0042311

Yes/No questions with *it's*

Question				Answer		
Is	**it**	an	eraser?	Yes, **it is**.	**It's** an eraser.	*It's = It is*
		a	pen?	No, **it isn't**.	**It's** a crayon.	*isn't = is not*

Is it *a clock? No,* ***it isn't. It's*** *a map.*

1 **Unscramble.** Write a question.

1. c c k o l clock Is it a clock?
2. p a m _____?
3. n l c p e i _____?
4. n e p _____?

2 **Look and read.** Write the answer.

1.  Is it a clock? Yes, it is.
2.  Is it a crayon? _____.
3.  Is it a map? _____.
4.  Is it a chair? _____.

3 **Write.** Look at Activity 2.

1. It's a clock.
2. _____.
3. _____.
4. _____.

4 **Look and write.**

1. ● It's a circle.
2. ★ _____.
3. ▲ _____.
4. ■ _____.

5 **Draw and write.** Draw a picture of your classroom. Write 2 questions and 2 answers.

_____

_____

_____

_____

What and *How many*

Question				Answer
What		is	it?	It's an eraser.
	color	is	it?	It's orange.

Question	Answer
How many erasers?	Three.

What asks about a thing. *How many* asks for a number.

1 **Read and match.** Draw a line.

1. Is it a	a. it?
2. It's an	b. picture?
3. What color	c. is it?
4. What is	d. papers?
5. How many	e. eraser.

2 **Read.** Write *What*, *What's*, or *How*.

1. _____ your name? I'm Sandy.
2. _____ color is it? It's purple.
3. _____ many pictures? Six.
4. _____ is it? It's a chair.

3 **Read and write.** Complete the questions.

1. What is it ? It's a book.
2. _____? It's black.
3. _____ chairs? Five.

4 Look and write.

1. 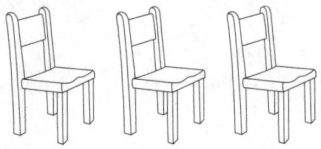

How many chairs _____?

Three _____.

2. 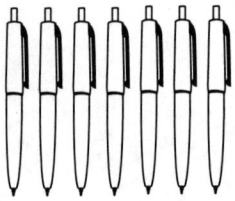

_____?

_____.

3. 

_____?

_____.

4. 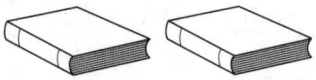

_____?

_____.

5 Write. Color the picture. Answer the questions.

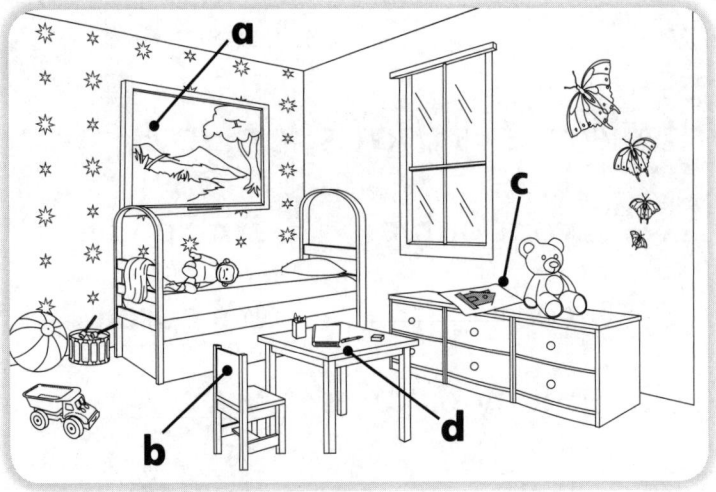

1. Look at **a**. What is it?

_____.

2. Look at **b**. What color is it?

_____.

3. Look at **c**. What is it?

_____.

4. Look at **d**. What color is it?

_____.

Unit 2

to be: is, are

Question			Answer		
What	**is**	it?	**It's**	a tree.	*It's = It is*
	are	they?	**They're**	trees.	*They're = They are*

one thing = ***It's*** *a bird*.

two or more things = ***They're*** *birds*.

1 Read. Circle the words.

1. **What** / **Is** it a river? Yes, it **is** / **are**.
2. What **is** / **are** it? It **'s** / **are** a butterfly.
3. What **is** / **are** they? They **is** / **are** trees.
4. **What** / **How** are they? **It's** / **They're** rocks.

2 Read. Rewrite the sentences.

1. It is a butterfly. It's a butterfly.
2. They are rocks. _____.
3. It is a bird. _____.
4. They are trees. _____.

3 **Look.** Write questions.

1. What is it _____?
2. _____?
3. _____?
4. _____?
5. _____?

4 **Look.** Answer the questions in Activity 3. Use the picture.

1. It's a cloud _____.
2. _____.
3. _____.
4. _____.
5. _____.

5 **Look and write.** Write 2 questions and 2 answers about the picture in Activity 2.

_____?

_____.

_____?

_____.

Where* and *in* or *on

Question			Answer
Where	is	the moon?	It's **in** the sky.
	are	the birds?	They're **on** the rock.

Use *in* or *on* + a place: ***in*** *the tree*, ***on*** *the bush*

1 Read. Circle the letter.

1. The clouds are _____ the sky. a. is b. on c. in
2. The rocks _____ in the river. a. is b. are c. on
3. The moon _____ in the sky. a. is b. on c. are
4. Where _____ the birds? a. is b. in c. are
5. The monkey is _____ the rock. a. in b. are c. on

2 Look. Write *in* or *on*.

1. The bird is _____ the tree.
2. The rocks are _____ the river.
3. The star is _____ the sky.
4. The bird is _____ the stick.

3 Look and write.

1. 

Where is the star? _____

2. 

_____?

3. 

_____?

4. 

_____?

4 Write. Answer the questions in Activity 3.

1. It's in the sky. _____

2. _____.

3. _____.

4. _____.

5 Look and write. Look outside. Write 3 questions and answers about what you see.

Where's the sun? It's in the sky. _____

_____

_____

_____

Unit 3

to have

Question	Answer			
How many sisters do you have?	I	**have**	one sister.	*don't = do not*
		don't have	any sisters.	

*I **have** one sister/two brothers.*

*I **don't have** any brothers.*

1 **Write.** Unscramble the sentences.

1. brother / have / a / I / big

   I have a big brother.

2. have / sister / a / I

   _____.

3. a / don't / brother / I / have

   _____.

4. parents / I / two / have

   _____.

2 **Read and write.** Give answers that are true for you.

1. Do you have _____ any sisters?

   _____.

2. How many parents _____?

   _____.

3. How many grandfathers _____?

   _____.

4. _____ any brothers?

   _____.

3 Look and write.

1. sister I don't have any sisters.
2. mother _____.
3. father _____.
4. brother _____.
5. grandfather _____.

4 Write. Write questions to ask a friend about family. Use the words in the box.

brother sister grandfather grandmother

1. Do you have a sister?
2. _____?
3. _____?
4. _____?

5 Write. Write 2 sentences about your family. Use *have*.

_____

_____

He/She and questions with *who*

Question		Answer	*Who's = Who is*
Who's	**he**?	**He's** my brother Jack.	*He's = He is*
	she?	**She's** my sister Ana.	*She's = She is*

Who asks about a person.

he = a boy/man *she* = a girl/woman

1 Look and write.

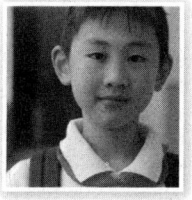

1. Who's he? 2. _____ 3. _____

2 Look and write. Imagine this is your family.

1.  Who's he? He's my brother. He's two.

2.  Who's she? _____. She's short.

3.  Who's he? _____. He's old.

4.  Who's she? _____. She's tall.

3 **Write.** Write questions and answers.

1. Who's he _____?

   He's my big brother. He's tall _____. (tall)

2. _____?

   _____. (young)

3. _____?

   _____. (ten)

4. _____?

   _____. (small)

4 **Draw and write.** Draw 2 people in your family. Then write about them. Use the words in the box.

old short tall young

_____

_____

_____

_____

Unit 4

Yes/No* questions with *Is there . . . ?

Question			Answer	
Is there	a lamp	in the bedroom?	Yes, **there is**.	*isn't = is not*
	a sofa	in the kitchen?	No, **there isn't**.	

Is there *a mirror in the kitchen? No,* ***there isn't****.*

1 Read. Look at your house. Circle the letter.

1. Is there a sofa in the bedroom?

   a. Yes, there is. b. No, there isn't.

2. Is there a clock in the kitchen?

   a. Yes, there is. b. No, there isn't.

3. Is there a chair in the living room?

   a. Yes, there is. b. No, there isn't.

4. Is there a lamp in the dining room?

   a. Yes, there is. b. No, there isn't.

2 Look and write.

1. Is there a sofa in the bedroom? No, there isn't.
2. _____ a lamp in the bedroom? _____.
3. _____ a clock in the bedroom? _____.
4. _____ a chair in the bedroom? _____.

3 **Look.** Write questions.

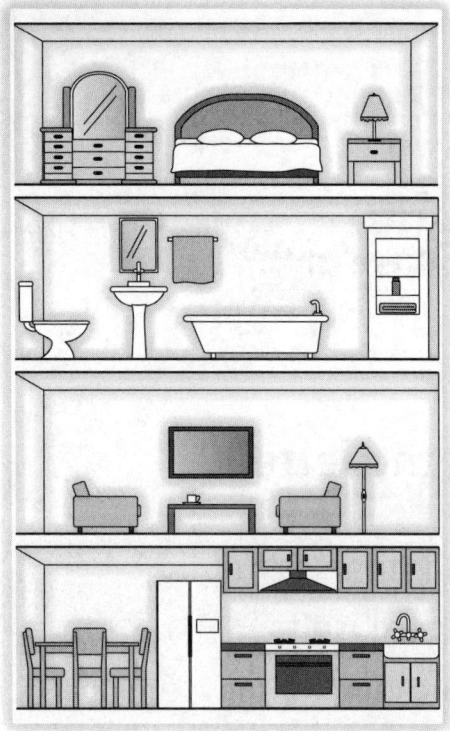

1. Is there a sofa in the bedroom?
2. _____?
3. _____?
4. _____?

4 **Write.** Answer your questions from Activity 3.

1. No, there isn't.
2. _____.
3. _____.
4. _____.

5 **Draw and write.** Draw your living room. Write 2 questions and answers.

_____
_____
_____
_____
_____

Present progressive: *He/She is* + verb-*ing*

Question	Answer
Where is your sister?	She's in the kitchen.

Question			Answer		
What's	she	**doing**?	She's	**eating**.	*What's = What is* *She's = She is*

do → doing *eat → eating*

1 Look and read. Circle the word.

1. 
She / She's eating.

3. 
He's / He taking a bath.

2. 
She's **sleeping** / **sleep**.

4. 
He's **watching** / **watch** TV.

2 Write. Rewrite the sentences. Use 's.

1. He is drawing. He's drawing _____.
2. She is singing. _____.
3. The baby is sleeping in the bedroom. _____
_____.
4. My brother is watching TV in the living room. _____
_____.

3 Look and write.

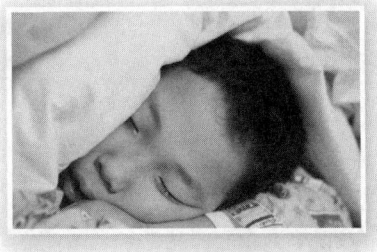

1. Where's your sister _____?

She's in the bedroom _____.

She's sleeping _____.

2. _____ your mother?

_____.

_____.

3. _____ your brother?

_____.

_____.

4. _____ your big sister?

_____.

_____.

4 Draw and write. Draw 2 family members at home. Write.

My father's in the kitchen.

He's cooking.

_____

_____

_____

_____

_____

_____

Unit 5

Present progressive: *am/are/is* + verb-*ing*

Question				Answer			
What	**are**	you	**wearing**?	I'**m**	**wearing**	white shoes.	*I'm = I am*
	is	your brother		He'**s**		a hat.	*He's = He is*
		the girl		She'**s**			*She's = She is*

You can also say:

*My mother'**s wearing** a hat. = My mother **is wearing** a hat.*

*The baby'**s wearing** a hat. = The baby **is wearing** a hat.*

1 Read. Circle.

1. What **is / are** she wearing?
2. What **is / are** you wearing?
3. **She's / She** wearing a red dress.
4. I **'m / 're** wearing gloves.
5. You **'s / 're** wearing socks.
6. I'm **wear / wearing** a skirt.

2 Write. Complete the questions on p. 18.

1. What is your mother wearing?

2. What _____ your brother _____?

3. What _____ your father _____?

4. What _____ you _____?

3 Color and write. Use Activity 2.

1. She's wearing green pants.

2. _____.

3. _____.

4. _____.

4 Look and write.

1. What is he wearing?
He's wearing pants.
He's wearing a shirt.

2. _____

3. _____

4. _____

You

Questions with *that* and *those*

Question		Answer		
What's	**that**?	**That**'s	my pink hat.	*What's = What is*
What are	**those**?	**Those** are	my brown pants.	*That's = That is*

that = one thing
those = two or more things/plurals

1 Look and read. Circle the words. Then match.

1.  What's **that** / **those**?
2.  What are **that** / **those**?
3.  What **'s** / **are** that?
4.  What **is** / **are** those?
5.  **What's** / **What are** that?

a. **That** / **Those** are my gloves.
b. **That's** / **Those** my hat.
c. **That's** / **Those** my skirt.
d. **That's** / **Those are** my socks.
e. That **'s** / **are** my shirt.

2 Write.

1. What's that _____? That's my blue dress.
2. _____? Those are my red gloves.
3. _____? Those are my black shoes.
4. _____? That's my white shirt.
5. _____? Those are my brown pants.

3 **Look and write.** Ask and answer questions.

1. What's that _____? That's my jacket _____.

2. _____? _____.

3. _____? _____.

4. _____? _____.

4 **Draw and write.** Draw and color a picture of your clothes. Choose 3 things. Write sentences.

_____

_____

_____

_____

Unit 6

Simple present of *want*: *I/you/he, she*

Question				Answer	
Do	you	**want**	a bike?	Yes, I **do**.	*don't = do not*
				No, I **don't**. I **want** a train.	
Does	he/she			Yes, he **does**.	*doesn't = does not*
				No, she **doesn't**. She **wants** a train.	

To ask a question: ***Do*** *you + want . . . ?* or ***Does*** *he/she + want . . . ?*

1 Read. Circle the words.

1. **Do** / **Does** you want a top? Yes, I **do** / **does**.
2. **Do** / **Does** he want a train? Yes, he **do** / **does**.
3. **Do** / **Does** she want a bike? Yes, she **does** / **doesn't**.
4. Do you **want** / **wants** a ball? No, I **don't** / **do**.

2 Read and write.

1. Does she ___want___ a kite?
2. _____ you want a truck?
3. He _____ a ball.
4. Does your brother _____ a top?
5. Do you _____ a train?
6. I _____ a bike.

3 **Read and write.** Answer the questions.

1. Do you want a game? _____.
2. Do you want a big car? _____.
3. Do you want a sister? _____.
4. Do you want a bike? _____.

4 **Look and write.**

1. 

   she / ☹

   Does she want a train _____?

   No, she doesn't _____.

2. 

   he / ☺

   _____?

   _____.

3. 

   he / ☹

   _____?

   _____.

4. 

   she / ☺

   _____?

   _____.

5 **Draw and write.** Draw 2 toys. Ask and answer questions with *want*.

_____?

_____.

_____?

_____.

Questions with *this* and *these*

Question		Answer	
Is **this**	your puzzle?	Yes, **it** is.	*isn't = is not*
		No, **it** isn't. **It's** Marco's puzzle.	*It's = It is*
Are **these**	your dolls?	Yes, **they** are.	*aren't = are not*
		No, **they** aren't. **They're** Anita's dolls.	*They're = They are*

For one thing:
*Is **this** your robot? Yes, **it** is.*

For two or more things:
*Are **these** your cars? No, **they** aren't.*

1 Read. Circle the words.

1. Is **this** / **these** your top?
   No, it **isn't** / **aren't**.
   It's / **They're** Juan's top.

2. Are these her **toy** / **toys**?
   No, they **aren't** / **isn't**.
   They're / **It's** my toys.

3. Are **this** / **these** your balls?
   Yes, **it** / **they** are.

4. **Are** / **Is** this your doll?
   No, **it** / **they** isn't.
   It's her **doll** / **dolls**.

2 Read and write. Complete the sentences.

1. _____ your robot?
   Yes, it _____.

2. _____ your puzzles?
   No, they _____. _____ Bob's puzzles.

3. _____ her teddy bear?
   No, it _____.

3 **Look and write.** Ask questions. Follow the model.

1. **Paolo's**

Is this your truck?

_____

2. **Carmen's**

_____

_____?

3. **Maya's**

_____

_____?

4. **Ava's**

_____

_____?

4 **Write.** Answer the questions in Activity 3.

1. No, it isn't. It's Paolo's truck.
2. _____.
3. _____.
4. _____.

5 **Write.** Write a conversation between friends about toys. Use the words in the box

aren't isn't these this

_____

_____

_____

_____

Unit 7

Possessive adjectives

I	have	black	hair.	**My**	hair	is	black.
You				**Your**			
He	has			**His**			
She				**Her**			

The sentences have the same meaning:

*I have blue eyes. = **My** eyes are blue.*

1 Look and read. Circle the word.

1. **His** / **Your** hair is black.
2. **His** / **Their** hair is black.
3. **Her** / **Their** hair is black.
4. **My** / **Our** hair is black.

   Your / **My** eyes are black, too!
5. This is my family.

   Our / **Your** hair is black.

4 You

2 Read and write. Use the words.

1. hair / short Her hair is short.

   eyes / black _____.
2. hair / short _____.
3. hair / black _____.

   eyes / black / too _____

   _____.

3 **Read.** Rewrite the sentences.

1. I have short hair. My hair is short _____.
2. My father has big ears. _____.
3. You have small hands. _____.
4. My grandmother and grandfather have white hair.

   _____.
5. My little sister has short legs. _____.
6. My baby brother has a small mouth. _____.

4 **Look and write.** Use *her, his, my,* and *your.*

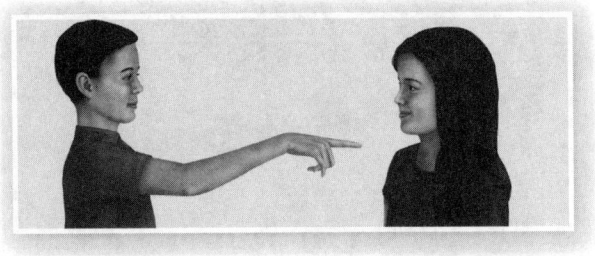

1. _____. (hair)

   _____. (eyes)

2. _____. (hand)

   _____. (nose)

5 **Write.** Find a photo of friends or family members. Put it here. Write 4 sentences about it.

Put photo here.

_____

_____

_____

_____

_____

Ability with *can*

I	**can**	draw.
He/She		

Question			Answer	
Can	you	draw?	Yes,	I **can**.
	he/she			he/she **can**.

Use *can* + action word: *I/you/he/she* ***can*** *cook*.

1 **Read and match.** Draw a line.

1. I can walk on my hands.
2. I can jump on one foot.
3. She can run and jump.
4. He can walk on his hands, too.

a. He has strong arms.
b. She has strong legs.
c. I have strong arms.
d. I have strong legs.

2 **Write.** Unscramble the words.

1. I / jump / can _____.
2. she / clean / can _____.
3. watch / he / can / TV _____.
4. big / can / my / sister / eat _____.
5. run / you / can _____?

3 **Look and write.** Write 3 sentences. Use *can*.

She can jump. _____

_____

_____

_____

4 **Look and write.** Write questions and answers.

1. 

Can you draw _____?

Yes, I can _____.

2. 

_____?

_____.

3. 

_____?

_____.

4. 

_____?

_____.

5 **Write.** Write 4 sentences about your friends or family. Use *can*.

My father can cook. _____

_____

_____

_____

_____

_____

Unit 8

***like* with count and noncount nouns**

Question				Answer	
Do	you	**like**	eggs?	Yes, I **do**.	*don't = do not*
				No, I **don't**.	
Does	he		soup?	Yes, he **does**.	*doesn't = does not*
				No, he **doesn't**.	

With *like*, say: *I* ***like*** *apples / bananas / eggs*. (Not: ~~*I like apple/banana/egg*~~.)
I ***like*** *soup*. (Not: ~~*I like soups*~~.)

1 Read. Circle your answer.

1. Do you like fish?
   a. Yes, I do. b. No, I don't.
2. Do you like apples?
   a. Yes, I do. b. No, I don't.
3. Do you like chicken?
   a. Yes, I do. b. No, I don't.
4. Do you like rice?
   a. Yes, I do. b. No, I don't.

2 Read. Write your answer.

1. Do you like computers? _____.
2. Do you like kites? _____.
3. Do you like robots? _____.
4. Do you like puzzles? _____.

3 Read and write.

1. Does he like sandwiches? No, he doesn't. He doesn't like sandwiches.
2. _____ you like oranges? Yes, I _____. I like oranges.
3. Does she _____ cookies? Yes, she does. She _____ cookies.
4. Do you _____ soup? No, I don't. I _____ like soup.
5. _____ she _____ eggs? No, she _____ like eggs.

4 Read. Write answers that are true for you.

1. Do you want a cookie? No, I don't. I don't like cookies.
2. Do you want some chicken? _____
3. Do you want an apple? _____
4. Do you want some rice? _____

5 Look and write. Write about people in your family.

1. 

   grandfather Does your grandfather like eggs?
   No, he doesn't. He likes chicken.

2. 

   mother _____

3. 

   brother/sister _____

4. 

   grandmother _____

Indefinite articles: *a, an*

a + consonant	banana, cookie, sandwich
an + vowel (a, e, i, o, u)	arm, eraser, orange

Use *a* or *an* with one thing: ***a*** *banana*, ***a*** *sandwich*, ***an*** *eraser*, ***an*** *orange*.
Don't use *a/an* with these words: *cheese, rice, soup, tea, water, milk, juice.*

1 **Write.** Make 2 lists.

~~apple~~ arm
banana computer
ear egg
eraser fish
mouth tree

a	an
	apple

2 **Read.** Write *a* or *an*.

1. Is it _____ pencil? No, it isn't. It's _____ table.
2. Is it _____ eraser? Yes, it is!
3. Is there _____ sofa in the living room? No, but there's _____ chair.
4. Does he want _____ apple? No. He wants _____ cookie.
5. There's _____ yellow butterfly. It's not _____ orange butterfly.

3 **Look and write.** Complete the sentences.

1. There is a girl, an _____, a _____, and an _____.
2. There isn't an _____, a _____, a _____, and an _____.

4 Look and write.

1.  a cookie

2.  _____

3.  _____

4.  _____

5.  _____

6.  _____

7.  _____

8.  _____

5 Write. Complete the sentences. Use all of the words.

~~map~~	chair	egg	eraser
old toy	~~apple~~	sofa	jacket

1. In my classroom, there isn't an apple.

   There is a map.

2. In my living room, there _____

   _____

3. In my kitchen, there _____

   _____

4. In my bedroom, there _____

   _____